R.

Annie Siddons

RAPUNZEL

OR

THE MAGIC PIG

OBERON BOOKS
LONDON

First published in 2006 by Oberon Books Ltd
521 Caledonian Road, London N7 9RH
Tel: 020 7607 3637 / Fax: 020 7607 3629
e-mail: info@oberonbooks.com
www.oberonbooks.com

A catalogue record for this book is available from the British
Library.

Cover design by Daryl Waller

ISBN: 1 84002 698 7 / 978-1-84002-698-6

Printed in Great Britain by Antony Rowe Ltd, Chippenham

For Bessie and Claudie with love

Forewords

On a blue-black, icy winter's night in 2003, in an isolated house in the Mendip Hills, I began to read the story of Rapunzel to my daughters. It was a bland retelling which I didn't think captured the horror, the passion or the intrigue of the story as I remembered it. But the image of Rapunzel's hair falling down like a curtain of light stayed with me and I began to wonder if I could work the story into a play.

Dismayed by the current fad for the Barbiefication of fairytales, and the hegemony of Disney, I turned to the master of saltiness and earthiness, Italo Calvino, for his fantastic versions of hundreds of folk tales, including many variants on the Rapunzel tale. I then went back further still, to Basile, the bawdy, irreverent first collector of folk tales in Italian. I read hundreds of variants – wildly different in detail but united by the herby name of the heroine, her va-va-voom, her cunning, and some sort of incarceration in a tower. I wanted my Rapunzel to have the wit, the sass, the spirit of these Basile and Calvino heroines. I wanted her journey to have real growth and suffering. I wanted her to actively choose the prince, not just go with him because he happened to hop into her tower. And I wanted her to be flesh and blood, not some odourless, laminated dollybird.

I'd seen Kneehigh's *The Red Shoes* at the Lyric Hammersmith and had thought – that's it, that's who I have to work with – but didn't expect anything to happen when I sent the first draft to Emma Rice in 2004. I'm amazed to be working with Kneehigh at BAC and in awe of their process and the direction in which they have helped me take the play.

Thanks to Emma, Mike, and everyone at Kneehigh, David Jubb and all at BAC, David Farr, Simon Reade, Italo Calvino and Giambattista Basile.

Annie Siddons

Human beings love stories. We love to get lost in a far off world, immersed in a cracking good narrative. Even as we become old and cracked, we still want and dream of the same things, we still ask the same questions, fear the same horrors… and folk tales are the deepest, darkest and truest of stories! This is why they have survived centuries and generations and telling upon telling. They hold a mirror up, not to our lives (for that, watch a soap opera), but to our souls. They talk to us about the most essential and painful parts of being alive – independence, freedom, loss and love. They teach us to listen to ourselves. As Schiller wrote:

> Deeper meaning resides in the fairytales told to me in my childhood than in the truth that is taught by life.

Kneehigh are storytellers. We believe in the power of the imagination and the live event. It is a delicious privilege to be able to bring Annie Siddons' mouth-wateringly magical telling of Rapunzel to life. Here's to joy and escape, fear and redemption and to giving in to the bliss of being told a great story.

Emma Rice
Artistic Director, Kneehigh Theatre

BAC and Kneehigh Theatre create an ideal partnership for the first production of Annie Siddons' joyful version of Rapunzel. In a research and development period for the production in April 2006 the scene with Patrizio, whom nature adores, and Paulo, whom nature torments, quickly became my favourite ever scene in theatre.

David Jubb
Artistic Director, BAC

Characters

UMBERTO
a peasant

RAPUNZEL
his daughter

MOTHER GOTHEL
a herbalist

MADDALENA

Maddalena's MOTHER

SIGNOR BALDOZI

MARIA

Maria's LITTLE BOY

The DUKE OF TUSCANY

PRINCE PATRIZIO
his son

PRINCE PAULO
his son

A BOAR / The PIG

LADDER-MAKER

PIERLUIGI AMBROSI
a ruffian

A TERRIFIED MAN

A LADY

ANOTHER TERRIFIED MAN

SHARK FANTINI
a black-clad villain

A SCIENTIST

A BEGGAR

A FISH WOMAN

A YOUNG WOMAN

An OLD MAN with a
wheelbarrow

A MAN

PREZZEMOLINA

SIGNOR FARFALLA
an adviser

A COOK

A PRIEST

A MAN WITH A PARCEL

A GOAT

A SNAKE

A CITIZEN

SERVANTS, CITIZENS,
RABBITS & GOATS

Rapunzel or *The Magic Pig* was first performed on 7 December 2006 at BAC, London, with the following company:

UMBERTO / PIERLUIGI AMBROSI, Paul Hunter
PATRIZIO, Pieter Lawman
MOTHER GOTHEL / PAULO, Mike Shepherd
RAPUNZEL, Edith Tankus
DUKE OF TUSCANY / SHARK FANTINI, James Traherne
PREZZEMOLINA, Kirsty Woodward
Musician Alex Vann

Director Emma Rice
Designer Michael Vale
Musical Director & Composer Stu Barker
Lighting Designer Alex Wardle

The text that follows was correct at the time of going to press and may differ slightly from the play as performed.

Act One

SCENE 1

Harsh, dry landscape. Quasi-desert. Wind blows parched earth. Everything's scorched. UMBERTO, a peasant in his fifties, enters with a baby. He walks. Whilst he walks he talks to her and she gurgles.

UMBERTO: There, there baby. That's right. That's right my lovely. Yes. Let's go along here a bit shall we?

UMBERTO falters. He is very out of breath.

Oh. I'm just going to stop and have a little, a little rest. That's right. Your dad's a bit unfit eh.

He pauses and catches his breath.

Okay. Let's carry on. I'm sure we can find somewhere soon. There there baby. It's okay.

Baby noises.

No, mama's not here darling. Mama's sleeping in the earth and there's no more milk for you. The goats had no more milk. I know you're thirsty baby. Oh is that sand in your face? Let's wipe it off, there.

He walks on, very hot.

Let's get you somewhere safe. Somewhere you will be looked after.

He is totally exhausted. Finally he reaches a place that looks promising. A beautiful garden. There are bees, butterflies and a sense of abundance and peace. Edenic. He pushes open the gate and lays his daughter down in the shade of a tree.

Oh look. Here. It's lovely here. This lovely green garden.

Tenderly he lays the baby down.

The garden will take care of you. I will never forget you. I love you.

The baby gurgles. UMBERTO limps off.

Garden music. From behind the trees, dressed in green, comes MOTHER GOTHEL, a sixty-year-old herbalist. She inspects her herb garden, picking this and that, talking to her plants. 'Hyssop's looking good. Oh, you're looking a bit straggly my darling, let's give you a bit of a prune. Oh, you've bloomed in the night, marvellous etc.' She finishes inspecting and then the baby cries. MOTHER GOTHEL is drawn to the cries.

GOTHEL: What's this? A miracle! Am I growing people now too?

She picks up the bundle.

A little girl! You can be *my* little girl! I will teach you all that I know. You will become a herbalist like me. And because I found you in the shade of the Rapunzel plant, you will be called Rapunzel.

She kisses and hugs the bundle lovingly and coos. It turns into a seven-year-old RAPUNZEL. The seven-year-old RAPUNZEL giggles and runs about, chasing butterflies. The place is idyllic. Idyllic music.

Rapunzel! Come here and help me grind up these seeds.

RAPUNZEL: (*Looking at a herb.*) What's that, Mother Gothel?

GOTHEL: That is Fairy's Spindle, my darling, though some call it Snake's Pie, and others call it Pandora's Pipes.

RAPUNZEL: What does it do?

GOTHEL: When you're tired and sad and lonely, it picks you up and turns you around again.

RAPUNZEL: And what about this one?

GOTHEL: That is hyssop, for coughs. We'll pick some and make an infusion. What you do is…take the leaves, the plumpest, biggest ones, that's right, leave the little ones, and then you boil them for thirty minutes.

RAPUNZEL: Thirty minutes.

GOTHEL: Off you go, and then we'll add some honey, because it's very bitter without.

RAPUNZEL: All right mother! See you in a bit.

She watches tenderly as RAPUNZEL goes off.

Time passes. A few years. RAPUNZEL is picking herbs. MOTHER GOTHEL watches. 'Herb-picking Song'

Rosemary, orach and thyme,
Parsley and sage and oregano,
Warmed by the sun and nourished by the rain
In our garden.

Hyssop and lovage and sage,
Wormwood and borage and vervain,
Stretch out their shoots to the morning,
And we tend them.

RAPUNZEL: (*Singing.*) Hmmm, hmmm, hmmmm, hmmmm.

Rosemary, for making dark hair shine. Camomile, for blondes. And parsley for mother's milk.

GOTHEL: You've become a talented herbalist, Rapunzel.

RAPUNZEL: Thank you mother. (*Kiss.*)

A woman in labour – MADDALENA – arrives with her MOTHER.

GOTHEL: You can do these ones.

RAPUNZEL: Really?

GOTHEL: Go on.

RAPUNZEL: (*Running to her.*) Ah, Maddalena, is it happening?

MOTHER: It's happening all right. She's been up all night, heeing and hawing like a donkey with toothache.

RAPUNZEL: Don't worry! Try and keep calm. In my basket I've got some tincture of costmary to soothe the pain.

She fetches the drink.

Drink this.

MADDALENA groans.

MOTHER: Thank you Rapunzel. It's her own fault for having a baby out of wedlock.

RAPUNZEL: The costmary will make it better. Breathe through the contractions. Good luck! Come and show me the baby! Bye!

GOTHEL: Bye!

MADDALENA and her MOTHER exit, a strange four-legged whimpering beast, just as a very old man – SIGNOR BALDOZI – arrives. The effort it must have taken him to leave his house and come here is unimaginable. Bent almost double, wheezing and limping, he strikes a comically pathetic figure.

RAPUNZEL: Signor Baldozi! How are you?

BALDOZI: Ah, Rapunzel. My rheumatism is killing me. My breath stinks like a dog. My scalp itches. How will I ever get Signora Maldini to marry me?

RAPUNZEL: (*Laughing.*) Let's see. Well, for your rheumatism, I have a poultice of horseradishes. For your breath, a decoction of parsley and caraway. For your hair, oil of rosemary. Take these and use them. And then how will Signora Maldini be able to resist you?

BALDOZI: Thank you my dear!

And off he shuffles to rest, just as a distraught woman, MARIA, arrives carrying her LITTLE BOY, who is limp and lifeless.

MARIA: Oh, Rapunzel! We was out in the hills with our sheep and little Giovanni just ran off after a butterfly and then next thing I know, he's lyin' on the floor bleedin' and shakin', says a wild dog came and bit him, now 'e starts salivating, he's all palsied, I fear the dog was the devil himself in disguise.

RAPUNZEL. Calm down Maria. Breathe, and chew on this. For your boy I'll make a tincture of black horehound. Give it to him every hour till he's calm. And Maria, don't worry. Everything will be fine.

She goes off to get the tincture, and MARIA and her LITTLE BOY exit.

RAPUNZEL and MOTHER GOTHEL coexist happily together. RAPUNZEL goes off to boil up some leaves.

A few years later...

SIGNOR BALDOZI comes back. He is unrecognisable. He's walking straight, with incongruously flamboyant new clothes and an attempt at a cocky swagger. He looks absurd but he is very happy.

BALDOZI: Buon giorno Mother Gothel!

GOTHEL: Hello signor. How is your wife?

BALDOZI: Oh, she's beautiful!

GOTHEL: How are the children?

BALDOZI: They are very well. In fact there's another one on the way!

GOTHEL: Number eight! Wonderful news!

BALDOZI: You have a very talented assistant there Gothel.

GOTHEL: I know.

BALDOZI: And I just wanted to ask her for, for…

GOTHEL: What?

BALDOZI: For a little tonic. My energy is not what it was, Mother Gothel.

MOTHER GOTHEL cackles dirtily.

GOTHEL: Rapunzel! Rapunzel!

RAPUNZEL arrives. She has changed again. She looks taller, curvier, more womanly. Her clothes are different. Her hair shines and is in plaits down to her waist. She's beautiful.

BALDOZI: (*Whistles.*) Well, well, well. It looks as if there's someone else's wedding night we should be thinking about, Mother Gothel.

GOTHEL: What?

BALDOZI: I mean Rapunzel, she is so, (*He indicates with his hands what she is like.*) she is, she is a woman now!

Suddenly the atmosphere in the garden changes. The birds stop singing. The bees stop buzzing. And MOTHER GOTHEL fixes SIGNOR BALDOZI with her deep green eyes and with such an intensity of gaze that SIGNOR BALDOZI, despite the newly found spring in his step, forgets to ask RAPUNZEL for the special herb to make him even more manly, and shuffles away. Garden music in sinister key.

RAPUNZEL: (*Quietly, tenderly.*) What is it mother?

GOTHEL: Come with me.

She takes her by the hand. They walk, and when GOTHEL has found the spot she wants –

Cut down those trees.

RAPUNZEL: Why?

GOTHEL: You'll see.

GOTHEL hands her the axe. RAPUNZEL cuts down some trees and brings logs cut into pieces.

Help me. That's it.

Together they construct a tower, getting higher and higher as they do so.

RAPUNZEL: What are we doing?

GOTHEL: You'll see.

Finally the tower is finished.

Right. In you go.

RAPUNZEL looks unsure but MOTHER GOTHEL shuts her in. MOTHER GOTHEL descends via RAPUNZEL's hair and leaves. RAPUNZEL has a look around, realises she can't escape, looks out of the window.

RAPUNZEL: Mother! Mother, what is this? Is it a new game? (*Ready to believe it is, then gradually unsure.*) Mother? Mother?

Then furious and frantic. Hammering.

Let me out! Let me out! Let me out! Mother! Let me out! Mother! Mother!

Enter MOTHER GOTHEL, carrying basket of books and food.

GOTHEL: Rapunzel! Rapunzel! Let down your long hair.

RAPUNZEL: Why? Why have you done this to me?

17

GOTHEL: Hush. Let down your hair and I'll explain.

RAPUNZEL stands and lets down her long hair. She hooks it round a hook and lets it fall to the ground. It is dazzling, like spun stars. MOTHER GOTHEL shins up the hair with her basket and climbs in through the window.

RAPUNZEL: Why have you locked me in this tower?

GOTHEL: Because I love you.

RAPUNZEL: You trap me because you love me?

GOTHEL: I want to keep you safe.

RAPUNZEL: But I'm in no danger!

MOTHER GOTHEL gives RAPUNZEL a pile of books and some food. She goes back out of the tower and makes a thick forest grow around it, just in case RAPUNZEL should get any ideas. RAPUNZEL is furious. She feels her soul grow sick. She tries to be calm, to find a way out. But it's no good. RAPUNZEL piles up books and stands on tiptoes trying to look out of the tiny window.

Mother! Mother! What are you doing? Somebody! Somebody! I'm here! Somebody! I'm here! Someone! Come! Come!

But no one ever comes except for MOTHER GOTHEL.

And every time RAPUNZEL asks her why she has locked her in the tower, the answer is the same, and after five years it is still the same.

Mother, why do you keep me here?

GOTHEL: Because I love you.

SCENE 2

Five years later. Tuscany. Courtly music. The two PRINCES OF
TUSCANY enter with their father, the DUKE. Bunting, flags,
hurrahs, photos etc. They reach the court. SERVANTS come and
present them with a cake which says '18' on it.

DUKE: Happy birthday my sons! What an exciting day for
us all. And now, bring the presents.

The presents are brought with stately ceremony.

For you, Paulo, this gun. It belonged to my grandfather.
It's made of rosewood inlaid with mother-of-pearl and
gold.

PAULO: Thank you father. I'll be sure to use it well. I'm
a great shot as you know. Remember those quails last
season? (*Makes rapid shooting noises.*) Didn't stand a
chance.

He plays with the gun.

DUKE: Yes. An excellent shot. Now. Patrizio. This
mandolin, made of pear wood for an especially
mellow sound, will I hope inspire you in your musical
compositions.

PATRIZIO: Thank you father, it's beautiful, look at the
engraving. I love it.

He starts to pluck it and invent a song. PRINCE PAULO
glowers at him.

DUKE: Now as you have reached your majority I must
tell you which of you is going to replace me as Duke of
Tuscany when I die.

PAULO / PATRIZIO: Father!

DUKE: Shhh. I want to put my house in order whilst I am
still vigorous and strong, so that I can enjoy my twilight

years with you both. I cannot run away from death you know. None of us can.

They look at him.

It's been hard for me to decide who will take my place. You have many attributes, and I'm proud of you both.

PAULO simpers expectantly.

Paulo, your learning is beyond that of any young man I have known. You grapple with concepts even I in my great age have difficulty understanding.

PAULO: Yes. I've made it my business to study the stars and planets, the machinations of the court, high finance, and matters of philosophy.

DUKE: Exactly.

PAULO: If you remember father, my tutor said I was the brightest star in the firmament. All his other pupils were as dull clods of earth compared to me.

DUKE: Indeed. But you are not content only with educating your mind are you.

PAULO starts preening and showing off.

PAULO: No father.

DUKE: You are strong too, strong as a bison.

PAULO: A lion. I won't stand for flabbiness, in either mind or body.

DUKE: May you continue to use your strength well.

PAULO: I will.

PAULO continues to show off, but PRINCE PATRIZIO is busy making up his song on his mandolin… 'Oh beautiful country dum dum dum'.

DUKE: Patrizio.

PATRIZIO: Yes father?

DUKE: You are my delight. Your generous nature, your kindness and sense of justice, your laughter, your music, have daily been my joy since you were born.

PATRIZIO: Thank you father!

DUKE: Patrizio, I'd like you to be my heir.

PAULO can't believe what he's hearing.

From now on you will wear this ring. It has been in our family since the sixteenth century and was made by the famous jeweller Reuben Goldschmidt. Promise me you'll always keep it close to your heart.

PAULO begins to doubt.

PATRIZIO: I promise.

The DUKE hands the ring over to PATRIZIO.

PAULO: Father! You're joking aren't you? I'm the clever one! I understand the court! I'm the strong one! Look!

DUKE: I love you both, very much. Don't take this decision as a sign that you are uncared for, Paulo. Respect it, because I'm your father. And now that you've reached your majority, you must go and explore the kingdom and beyond, see what you make of it. Go! Find out things! Meet people! Enjoy yourselves!

He forces them into a hug.

PATRIZIO: Come on!

He leads out, plucking his mandolin. PAULO follows, furious. The DUKE watches them go.

Now they go on their Grand Tour. For PATRIZIO, it's a thing of wonder and delight. PAULO sees only darkness.

Look, it's the Sistine Chapel! Look at the workmanship on that! It's stunning! How did he do that bit? He must have really cricked his neck!

PAULO: It's just vulgar showing off.

PATRIZIO: Oh, and look over there, there's a lovely girl selling cheeses. Let's go and try some! Hello! Can I try some of your cheese?

PAULO: Peasant food.

PATRIZIO: Paulo, look at that wonderful building, it's leaning over towards us. How fascinating! Oh and you can get your portrait painted with you holding it up! That's great! Let's get it done! Signor! A portrait!

PATRIZIO poses by the Leaning Tower. PAULO does not.

PAULO: Can we go now?

They walk on and eventually come to a lovely pastoral scene.

PATRIZIO: We've had such incredible adventures, and it's so peaceful here. Let's sit down a while.

PAULO grudgingly sits down. PATRIZIO plucks and composes his song whilst RABBITS, birds and all of nature flock about him benevolently. PAULO has the opposite experience. Nature seems to be torturing him.

What do you think of this verse?

Oh beautiful country,
Your roads I am wandering,
My heart's full of yearning
To find my true love.
Hmmm hmmm
Hmmmm hmmmm.

(*Chorus.*) Road will you take me,
Wind will you blow,

Stars won't you light me
Over the plain
To ease my heart.

Oh branches and treetops,
I hear you are sighing,
Have you seen her the one
I am destined to love?

Chorus.

Oh tiny bird singing,
Your song will awake her,
Her heart will be soaring
When she feels my love.

Chorus.

PAULO glowers. He covers his ears, grimaces etc. when PATRIZIO plays. PATRIZIO is innocently oblivious. After being stung by midges, being bitten by PSYCHO-RABBITS, treading in shit, feeling the sun as a sadistic and infernal power, finally being able to take no more, PAULO gets out his gun and puts it to PATRIZIO's back. PATRIZIO turns.

What are you – ?

PAULO: I've always hated you. Always.

PATRIZIO: Why?

PAULO: Just you. Your happy nature. Your kindness. Your – *music.* I hate it all.

PATRIZIO: But brother –

PAULO has his gun to PATRIZIO's chest. PATRIZIO grabs it. Suddenly a huge BOAR charges through the forest squealing. It seems to be saying 'Murderer! Murderer!' The noise shocks PAULO so much that he drops his gun and runs away.

(*Following.*) Come back – explain to me. What have I done to you?!! Come back!

23

He walks off searching for him. He enters a forest. RAPUNZEL's lament begins.

RAPUNZEL: Libertà, libertà, libertà, libertà.

PATRIZIO sings his song over. The other actors are the forest. Branches tug at his hair and his clothes. Thorns tear at his skin. It is as if no one has ever walked there before.

PATRIZIO: Paulo! (*Looking for him.*) Paulo! Paulo! Come back! It's okay! He's gone. He must be jealous. If only he knew I'd share everything with him!

He walks further and further into the forest. The trees rip at his clothes until he is dressed in rags and unrecognisable as a prince.

Look at me now, Paulo, no one would think I am a prince and heir to the Duchy of Tuscany!

Sad, angry singing in the distance. He follows the sound and stumbles into a clearing. It is now night-time, and the sky is gloriously pinpricked with stars. RAPUNZEL's lament.

RAPUNZEL: Libertà! Libertà! Libertà!

RAPUNZEL sings her song loud and clear into the night. As she does so –

PATRIZIO: What wonderful music. But how sad. Who could be singing up there? A spirit? There's no door to the tower. Only a tiny window.

PATRIZIO tries to walk round the tower, but the thorny bushes prevent him. He hacks away at them with his sword, but they grow back again more thickly than ever.

How can anyone get in there? I'm going to lie down here, and watch and wait and see if someone comes out.

He does so.

Dawn breaks, and with it comes MOTHER GOTHEL, bearing a basket of bread and fruit for RAPUNZEL. She stoops down, picks a bit of herb, sniffs it, rubs it in her hands and flosses her teeth with it.

GOTHEL: Rapunzel, Rapunzel, let down your long hair!

PATRIZIO stirs and looks. Instantly the hair comes down, a waterfall of light.

PATRIZIO: (*From his hiding place, sotto voce.*) So beautiful! Is it really hair?

MOTHER GOTHEL climbs the hair.

(*Getting closer to have a better look.*) A ladder of hair! I must see who is up there. When the old hag comes down and night falls, then it's my turn.

MOTHER GOTHEL climbs down the hair with her empty basket. The hair is hauled in. PATRIZIO watches with bated breath. A nightingale sings, then all is quiet. Night falls. RAPUNZEL starts to sing her song again.

Right. What did she do first?

Audience may respond.

She picked something.

PATRIZIO picks herb, but nothing happens.

Then what. Ah yes, she sniffed it. Hmm.

Audience responds – hopefully.

She rubbed it in her hands – that's right – and then she flossed her teeth with it. Ugh. Bitter. Right.

Nothing happens.

And then she called to the person up in the tower. What did she say?

AUDIENCE: 'Rapunzel! Rapunzel! Let down your hair!'

PATRIZIO: Oh, right. Okay. I'd better do it in the old woman's voice. (*In an old woman's voice.*) Rapunzel! Rapunzel! Let down your long hair!

RAPUNZEL stirs and wakes up. The hair comes down. PATRIZIO goes up.

In RAPUNZEL's tiny tower, PATRIZIO is hauling himself through the window. As he does so, the hair shrinks back to a reasonable length. RAPUNZEL has her back to the window.

RAPUNZEL: Mother, you're heavy tonight – why have you come in the middle of the night?

She turns angrily.

Oh!

She is felled by the sight of another human being. He is transfixed by her beauty.

Oh!

She's completely shocked at the sight of another person and backs off.

PATRIZIO: (*Somewhat ineffectually, he's so awestruck.*) It's okay. I mean you no harm.

RAPUNZEL: (*Slowly getting up and collecting herself.*) Who are you? Why are you here?

PATRIZIO: I'm Patrizio. I heard your song. It was beautiful.

RAPUNZEL looks at him mistrustfully and continues to back away.

No it's true, it's true, I'm Patrizio, Pat-ri-zi-o, I was out with my brother in the fields, and we got separated and I was looking for him. I went into the forest to find him and I was drawn towards the tower by the sound of your voice. Please believe me. It's true. It's really true.

RAPUNZEL: Really.

PATRIZIO: Yes.

RAPUNZEL: (*Suddenly relaxing.*) I'm Rapunzel. I live in this tower. I don't know when I'm going to get out.

PATRIZIO: Who's the old woman?

RAPUNZEL: She's my mother.

PATRIZIO: Your mother? Why's she locked you away?

RAPUNZEL: Because she loves me!

PATRIZIO: That's not love!

RAPUNZEL: I know!

They stand there staring at each other, facing each other off. RAPUNZEL has forgotten how to converse.

After some while…

Um, ah. Conversation. I've been alone too long. Patrizio, where do you come from?

PATRIZIO: Tuscany.

RAPUNZEL: Ah, Tuscany. What's it like, Tuscany?

PATRIZIO: It's beautiful. There are great cities, and gentle green hills, and wonderful light.

RAPUNZEL: Can you live well there?

PATRIZIO: Very well. There are vineyards and fresh fruits growing and olive groves. And you? How have you been passing the time in this tower?

RAPUNZEL: I've been trying to educate myself. I've been teaching myself to read – I'm very learned now. Before I just knew about herbs. The only reason I haven't gone completely mad is that Hagface allows me to read.

Do you know this book? I like this one, it's one of my favourites.

She reads from a book of natural science.

PATRIZIO: Oh, really, manatees can live in saltwater *and* freshwater, that's fascinating, I didn't know that.

From a book of philosophy.

That's quite controversial isn't it – is it the egg or the chicken that came first? Which is ontologically prior?

From a book of sociology.

Romantic love is a myth designed to perpetuate the economic status quo. No. I don't agree with that. Definitely…not

They kiss. You can almost see neon hearts in the air: ping, ping, ping. Such is the energy of their love transferring from one to another. 'Ping Ping Song':

Ping ping, when my heart went boom
Ping ping, when you walked in the room
Ping ping, when I touched your skin
Ping ping, you make me wanna sing
Ping ping, skin skin, sing sing, I wanna ping-a-ling
    with you.

Yeh yeh yeh yeh yeh
Yeh yeh

Shubedebop, I wanna climb to the top
Shubedebop, I can't ever stop
Shubedebop, I wanna touch your hair
Shubedebop, they make a lovely pair
Shubedebop, can't stop, touch hair, where do we go
    from here?

Yeh yeh yeh yeh yeh
Yeh yeh

Zip zip, let's go hip to hip
Zip zip, you've got the softest lips
Zip zip, when I heard your song
Zip zip, I felt compelled to come
Zip zip, hip hip, soft lips
I wanna kkkkk-kiss you again.

AUDIENCE: Ping ping, boom boom, zip zip, sugar sugar.

Reluctantly they part then sit together.

RAPUNZEL: Oh. It's morning. I can feel the sun's heat on the stone. You've got to go!

PATRIZIO: I'm not leaving without you.

RAPUNZEL: Mother will kill you if she finds you.

PATRIZIO: Isn't there another way down?

RAPUNZEL: No.

PATRIZIO: How about a ladder?

RAPUNZEL: Do you know of a ladder long enough to reach up here? And light enough for you to carry in your pocket?

PATRIZIO: I'll find one.

RAPUNZEL: You think you can?

PATRIZIO: Of course!

RAPUNZEL: Now go.

He makes to go, but –

PATRIZIO: I don't want to leave you.

RAPUNZEL: It's only for a while. Patrizio! Don't forget the ladder. Don't forget!

With some panache, he swings himself out of the window, on the hair ladder.

PATRIZIO: I won't. Rapunzel, take this ring. My father gave it to me, and made me promise to keep it close to my heart. To obey him, I will have to give it to you.

He takes the ring from his finger and gives it to her.

RAPUNZEL: I will never lose it. Hurry back Patrizio.

PATRIZIO: I will.

He is about to disappear down the hair ladder.

One more kiss.

RAPUNZEL: Yes.

PATRIZIO goes.

Come back Patrizio! Let's kiss again, and then take me away to your land where the olives grow. Come soon! Give me love! Give me freedom!

Then, thinking –

I must make sure mother doesn't find out. I must be vigilant. Heart, do not betray me! Do not beat fast thinking of him! Stay calm. Ring, you are my Patrizio until the real one comes again, so you must lie next to my heart.

She conceals the ring in her bosom.

Time passing sequence. Freeze of MOTHER GOTHEL chatting to RAPUNZEL. RAPUNZEL reading. RAPUNZEL staring. RAPUNZEL dreaming of PATRIZIO and clutching the ring.

Music. PATRIZIO runs about the stage, looking for rope ladder-makers. He knocks on various doors, asks for a very long, very light ladder to be made, but to no avail, all the ladder-makers say no or get angry and slam the door in his face. Finally, out of breath, he comes across a tiny, secret door with the sign of a ladder outside it. He knocks on it.

PATRIZIO: Hello, I'm Patrizio, I need a rope ladder that I can fit into my pocket, that is as light as air but a hundred metres long.

LADDER-MAKER beckons PATRIZIO into his workshop, where he does many complex calculations and diagrams.

LADDER-MAKER: It will take me three weeks.

PATRIZIO: Brilliant.

PATRIZIO dashes back to the South.

Rapunzel! Rapunzel! Let down your long hair!

RAPUNZEL does so. PATRIZIO climbs up.

Rapunzel!

They kiss. With some fervour. During the following angry exchange they still can't help kissing.

RAPUNZEL: Where is it? Where's the ladder?

PATRIZIO: I've got good news. I've found someone who can make us a ladder!

RAPUNZEL: I don't understand.

PATRIZIO: It'll be ready in just three weeks!

RAPUNZEL: Three weeks! You came here to tell me I have to stay here another three weeks? That's not love! That's sadism! I've been here for five years! Five years I have seen nothing but these walls! You knew that! Now go! Don't come back any more unless you can get me out of here!

PATRIZIO: But Rapunzel –

RAPUNZEL: *Don't* talk to me!

PATRIZIO: But Ra –

RAPUNZEL: I can't believe you dared to come back!

PATRIZIO: But R –

RAPUNZEL: No, don't come back again unless you have the ladder for me! Go! Now! Go on! And Don't Pull My Hair!

PATRIZIO goes, somewhat surprised at her personality change.

(*Beyond herself with rage and incomprehension.*) Can I trust no one? No one apart from myself?

GOTHEL: (*Off.*) Rapunzel! Rapunzel! Let down your long hair!

RAPUNZEL: What now?

RAPUNZEL does so. MOTHER GOTHEL enters.

Oh it's you! I should have known from how light you were, you scrawny old hag.

GOTHEL: (*Incandescent.*) What? So what else has been climbing up your hair?

RAPUNZEL: No one you know.

MOTHER GOTHEL slaps her and she falls to her chair. MOTHER GOTHEL very slowly gets out her scissors. RAPUNZEL is too scared to move. Very slowly MOTHER GOTHEL begins to snip, snip. 'Snip Snip' music starts. Very gently she says:

GOTHEL: I loved you. (*Snip snip.*) I taught you all I knew. (*Snip.*) I passed on all my precious knowledge. (*Snip snip.*) I wanted to keep you safe. I would have let you out when I knew you were safe. (*Snip snip.*) You have hurt me so much my darling. You have disappointed me.

RAPUNZEL cries.

Now weave this hair into a plait.

RAPUNZEL weaves, sobbing.

Now go. You think you're a big girl now. You think you know what love is. You see, out in the world, if you know what love is. You go and see. Goodbye Rapunzel.

RAPUNZEL: Mother!

RAPUNZEL descends, looking up at MOTHER GOTHEL.

'Snip Snip Song':

> Hair in my hand let it fall to the floor;
> Cut off her hair she's a girl no more.

Three weeks later...

PATRIZIO enters jauntily, whistling, with a large rope ladder.

PATRIZIO I'm so in love! My heart is bursting. I keep wanting to hug everyone. I keep brushing my teeth with my mandolin and trying to play my toothbrush. She's so incredible! I've got the ladder in my pocket, and so today's the day! We're going to rush back to my father's kingdom and get married! Rapunzel! Rapunzel! Let down your long hair!

The hair comes down.

I can't wait to show her the ladder!

Eagerly, bursting with love, he shimmies up the hair, until he can see into the tower. MOTHER GOTHEL is in the tower.

Oh!

GOTHEL: There's no love greater than a mother's love. You thought she was there for the taking, but you were wrong. She's gone. She ran away. She felt guilty. And dirty.

PATRIZIO: Where is she?

GOTHEL: She left three weeks ago. She left a note, hang on, where is it?

She pretends to look for it but actually gets her scissors and blinds PATRIZIO.

PATRIZIO: Can I help you – aaaaaaaaah!

She takes the ladder from him, then leads him to the window where the hair is.

GOTHEL: Now you see if you can find her, eh?

PATRIZIO heaves himself down the hair, in considerable pain. MOTHER GOTHEL plants PATRIZIO's eyes into a pot, and they grow into a bush with a thousand eyes.

For as long as you live, little plant, I will know that he lives. I'll be watching you and hoping you will shrivel and die before long. No one steals my Rapunzel and lives happily ever after. Who said that herbalists have to be healers? When the season changes, you have to change your ways.

End of Act One.

Act Two

PROLOGUE

Three months later. A group of wealthy people, blindfolded, faces frozen into expressions of terror, glued together for comfort, huddles into the room. A man – PIERLUIGI AMBROSI – with a bag over his head and a gun in his hand, is moving them along.

AMBROSI: Move along now please, that's right, move along.

The group scuttles into a corner.

Right now. We appear to have a little problem. I'm supposed to be protecting you from the roguish and unsavoury elements that have appeared in the city since Prince Patrizio's disappearance. Is that right?

Terrified noddings and murmurs of assent, 'Yes signor, yes signor, that's right, yes, yes', from the group of wealthy people.

And yet we seem to have encountered resistance in ourselves. Resistance! Now that makes me a bit irritated. Why resist? Everyone knows it's easier to go with the flow. So. For those of you with memories shorter than your promissory-note-writing arms, let me remind you. The deal was this. What was the deal, actually, Signor Santi?

TERRIFIED MAN: (*In tiny voice.*) We pay, you protect.

AMBROSI: That's right. Now a little louder, for your hard-of-hearing friends.

TERRIFIED MAN: We pay, you protect.

AMBROSI: That's right. Now, what's been happening lately that has meant I haven't been able to protect you in

ANNIE SIDDONS

the way I might have liked to? Anyone? You, Signora
Rosselini.

LADY: We haven't been paying you.

AMBROSI: Anyone not hear that? You haven't been paying
me. And what do you think the consequences of that
might be. It's a no-brainer, really. Anyone?

ANOTHER TERRIFIED MAN: You won't protect us?

AMBROSI: Hurrah! You're all on terribly good form today.
I can't protect if you won't pay. It's that simple. So let's
all try a little game shall we now. Everybody dig deep
deep deep into their pockets and see what they can
find. And I'm not interested in your lucky feathers, your
special pennies, your magic buttons.

*The terrified burghers dig into their pockets and throw out
money. Sometimes it's in purses, sometimes it's loose.*

Good, that's lovely Signora Fellini. A fine purse you
have there. Oh, well done Signor Cavalieri. That is nice.
Thank you. You're all getting the hang of it. Well done.

*AMBROSI paces up and down with an air of impatience.
Suddenly, another man in a mask, SHARK FANTINI, comes
up behind him, pointing a gun.*

SHARK: Ambrosi!

AMBROSI: Who wants me?

SHARK: Shark Fantini. You're scum, Ambrosi. You're a
has-been. Get out of the city before I turn your skin into
gloves!

*SHARK FANTINI strikes AMBROSI on the head with his
pistol and runs off with the money, shooting into the air. The
terrified burghers disperse.*

*Slowly AMBROSI comes to and soon realises what has
happened...*

AMBROSI: Oh, fettuccine.

He sits up. Music: pling pling pling pling – doomcha-doomcha-doomcha – kind of Italianish music.

Blimey. All sorts has been going on here in Tuscany. Since the Prince Patrizio was chased through the forest by a ferocious wild boar three months ago, the Duke, normally as sane and wise a ruler as any blue-blood could be, has poured all the royal money into financing complicated expeditions to find him. (*Feels bruise.*) Ouch. Anyway, the royal money is rapidly running out and the Duke has to keep printing money, borrowing money from other princes, and raising taxes. As a consequence, prices are soaring, and people are beginning to starve. F'rinstance, how much do you think this stylish *cappello* would be, normally?

Takes suggestions from audience.

Very good yes. That's right. It's normally about fifty lire. But how much do you think it is now?

Takes suggestions.

Oh, no no darling, you're way off. No, double it. Then Triple it. Thassiright. Then multiply it by ten. Yes. You may well gape like a fish. This stunning headpiece now costs forty million lire. Beggars belief doesn't it! Times are hard. No doubt about it. Anyway, as a result of this insane inflation, the starving masses are getting naughty. Stealing, looting, raiding. Not pleasant. Not a lot of finesse in a starving mob, know what I'm saying? So that's where I come in. I look after the rich. Protect them. And they pay me. It's a win-win situation. Has anyone got any herbs for a headache? I'm seeing millions of you, everywhere. Lights dancing, everything. It's quite mesmerizing actually.

Only thing is, although I was – am – arch-villain, arch-controller, arch-lad, the more desperate people become, the more naughty they become, and now there are gangs running about everywhere, setting up their own protection rackets and whatnot, even though it was my idea. Nightmare I'm telling you. Ow. Can you see the bruise coming up there? I used to have the run of this place, now I have to watch my behind. I'm even considering leaving my beloved city walls for the first time ever, go and live the quiet life in the countryside; goats, tomatoes, aubergines.

SCENE 1

In the palace. There is a map of 'The South' marked with the forest and possible sightings of the pig.

DUKE: What news?

SCIENTIST: S-s-s-ire, much as we have had encouraging signs, it has still unfortunately been impossible for us to find either the pig or the prince.

DUKE: Then go. Redouble your efforts. Spare no expense.

He chucks handfuls of notes at the SCIENTIST, who grapples to pick them up and exits sycophantically.

PAULO: Father, I'm concerned and must speak frankly. Your obsession with finding Patrizio has led to much suffering in this land. You must turn your attention homewards. If, heaven forbid, Patrizio is dead –

DUKE: Thank you, Paulo, you mean well. But I am so convinced that Patrizio is alive that I promise you this. If, after all, I am proven wrong – if I have proof beyond a doubt that my son is dead, I will abdicate. You will have to rule in my place.

The DUKE leaves.

PAULO: (*To self.*) 'If I am proven wrong, if I have proof beyond a doubt that my son is dead, I will abdicate, and you will have to rule in my place.' Of course. 'Proof that my son is dead.' Ha. Some subtle machinations are needed, then the duchy and all its glory, power and magnificence will be mine. Which is no less than I deserve. And who better to help me than that mealy-faced scoundrel Pierluigi Ambrosi? What sport we shall have...

He picks up a pen and writes.

SCENE 2

Scrubby, bare countryside. RAPUNZEL, utterly filthy, her hair short and matted, her dress soiled and in tatters, her feet bare, enters through the audience.

RAPUNZEL: Patrizio! Patrizio! Where are you? Please forgive me. My soul is sick with the lack of you. I'll find you before mother gets to you, before she hurts you with her jealous heart.

A grey, grim family, thin and emaciated, scurry past, carrying all their wordly possessions in a wheelbarrow.

Excuse me! Hello! I'm looking for someone called Patrizio.

The family turns like ghosts to look at her, then scurries on.

Hello! Where are we?

No answer. Silence.

What's wrong with everyone? Patrizio! Patrizio!

RAPUNZEL is about to feel sorry for herself. But then the huge BOAR from earlier comes ambling along. It is magnificent.

What are you? Some kind of pig!

The PIG cocks its head and looks at her.

You're beautiful!

The PIG stands still in the middle of the road. Then it does a huge turd. Then, with its snout, it pushes the turd towards RAPUNZEL.

Thanks?

The PIG is insistent.

You want me to have this?

The PIG nods.

I don't know what to say.

The PIG nuzzles the turd towards RAPUNZEL.

Thank you.

Gingerly she picks up the turd and it opens to reveal three acorns.

Do I eat them?

The PIG shakes its head.

Good. Good. I don't eat them. I plant them?

The PIG shakes its head. It moves its leg in a throwing gesture.

What then? I throw them?

The PIG nods.

Now?

The PIG shakes its head. With its hoof on the ground it acts out 'Danger' in the style of a charade. RAPUNZEL guesses what the PIG is trying to act. A few wrong guesses, then:

I throw them down when I'm in danger!

The PIG nods.

Thank you. Can you tell me, am I going in the right direction?

The PIG draws a crown in the dust.

A crown… So I am to go to the palace, and ask about him. Perhaps he works there!

RAPUNZEL wraps the acorns up carefully and puts them in her pocket.

Thank you.

The PIG condescends to be stroked before trotting off.

Right mother. See if my love doesn't last.

Then she walks off.

SCENE 3

The palace. PRINCE PAULO and PIERLUIGI AMBROSI with bandaged head.

AMBROSI: What can I do for you?

They huddle secretively.

PAULO: When we reached our majority, father decided it was time he announced which of us would be his heir. And he chose Patrizio.

AMBROSI: Really.

PAULO: Yes. He also presented him with a ruby ring. A ring which has been in the family for four hundred years. Exquisitely wrought in gold and ruby, with the family crest of an eagle inscribed within, the ring was made by one Reuben Goldschmidt in the sixteenth century.

AMBROSI: (*Whistles.*) *The* Reuben Goldschmidt?

PAULO: Yup: it's the most valuable of all father's possessions, irreplaceable, and when he was given it, Patrizio promised it would always stay close to his heart.

AMBROSI: Bless.

The DUKE passes through with his advisor SIGNOR FARFALLA, who is carrying plans.

PAULO: Hello father.

DUKE: I've decided to borrow some money off the Duke of Puglia.

PAULO: Father that's not a very sensible idea, you've –

DUKE: I must find Patrizio. My life is utterly meaningless without him.

He goes out.

PAULO: You see he's quite insane. And now he's said that if he can prove Patrizio is dead, he'll abdicate, and I'll become Duke.

AMBROSI: You clever little princeling! The classic overthrow-your-own-father plot!

PAULO: So all I need you to do is to find Patrizio, kill him, present father with the ring, and then all will be well.

AMBROSI: Is that all?

DUKE enters again.

DUKE: Paulo have you seen my seal?

PAULO: Your seal? It's on your desk father. Behind your miniature lemon tree.

DUKE: Is it? Oh. I couldn't see it. I can't seem to find things these days. Everything slips away from me. Everything vanishes.

PAULO: I'll be right in to help you find it, once I've finished discussing the shooting party with this gentleman.

DUKE: What? Oh no, I'm sorry Paulo that's out of the question. There will be no shooting party this year.

PAULO: No?

DUKE: We can't divert money away from the search for your brother. Absolutely not. I need it all for my expeditions.

PAULO: I see. I'll be in presently father.

DUKE: Thank you Paulo. Now my seal, where did I put it?

He exits again.

PAULO: You see how insane he is. His brains have flown the coop.

AMBROSI: Yes, they do seem to have fluttered off. Let's hope it's not hereditary.

PAULO: Now. I suppose you're not going to do this for me out of the goodness of your heart.

AMBROSI: (*Considers.*) It's a high-risk operation. And going out of the city as well, you know I hate doing that. I hope you've taken all this into account.

PAULO: I'm offering you six bags of gold.

AMBROSI: It breaks my heart to turn you down sire.

PAULO: Eight.

He rises to leave.

AMBROSI: I love to be a port in a storm, but –

PAULO: All right then you scoundrel! I'll give you ten: four now, six after.

43

He fetches gold from a casket.

AMBROSI: That's more like it. Make it even-Stephens and I'll do it.

DUKE: (*Off.*) Paulo! Paulo! I still can't find it!

PAULO quickly hides gold as the DUKE approaches.

AMBROSI: Very nice. I'll try not to disappoint.

DUKE: You still here? There's absolutely no question of a shooting party I'm afraid.

AMBROSI: No I appreciate that sire. Just leaving sire.

DUKE: Paulo –

PAULO: I'll be right along father.

DUKE: Don't be long.

PAULO: I won't.

DUKE leaves. PAULO hands over gold. AMBROSI takes it appreciatively.

AMBROSI: Right then, I'll be off.

PAULO: Good. Now. Ambrosi, make sure you succeed, hmm? I hear Shark Fantini is a good shot.

SCENE 4

PATRIZIO, blind, with stick, still carrying mandolin, is in another part of the country. RAPUNZEL walks in another area of the stage.

PATRIZIO: Rapunzel. Rapunzel! Even if you can't hear me, I hope you know that you're in my thoughts all the time. Please keep safe, I'm coming to find you.

> Road won't you take me
> Wind will you blow

Hmm mmmm hmmmmm
Hmmm hmmm hmmm

I will wander the entire surface of the earth until I find you. Who needs eyes? I still have ears, hands, and a heart that yearns for you.

He walks. A BEGGAR is sitting in the road. Sees PATRIZIO and perks up.

BEGGAR: Lord have mercy upon me Christ have mercy upon me Lord have mercy upon me Christ have mercy upon me.

PATRIZIO: Poor wretch. I have no food but here, have my cloak.

He hands the BEGGAR his raggedy cloak. The BEGGAR jumps up and beats him, and steals his mandolin. He kicks him and walks off.

Why are you doing this? Why do you need to do this? You can take everything, but you can't take away my love. I'll go on to the ends of the earth, to the end of time.

SCENE 5

Sign: 'City: 60 km. Sea: 10 km'

AMBROSI: (*Eating calzone and carrying bottle of wine and dessert.*) Blimey. I've been all over Italy, from Brindisi to Milano, from Trieste to Palermo, and now I'm in this dump. Niente. Nobody has seen or heard of the exquisite ruby ring and I am footsore, stinking, and weary. If only five bags of gold were enough to buy my smallholding, I'd be off like a shot. Wouldn't bother to deliver. But prices are so high, you can't even get a mangy old shed for five bags of gold. So my fealty to that wormy prince is bought. It's not good for the soul.

45

He eats and drinks pensively.

But today, sweet oblivion. I am not doing a single thing. I deserve a day off.

He drinks heavily.

Hmmm that's good. That's goooood. Sweet nectar of the gods.

He walks on a bit.

Couple of goats, I'll learn how to make cheese. The simple life. Waking up in the morning, knowing I am my own boss and no one is after my behind. That's what I call living. Yessssssssss.

He falls down dead drunk in a ditch. RAPUNZEL enters and stumbles along. She is very hungry. Her stomach hurts.

RAPUNZEL: Spaghetti bolognese, garlic, and tomatoes. Sweet, juicy nectarines. Soup with beans and meat. The smell of bread. The first melon.

She gets out her acorn and looks at it.

I could use my acorn… I could use it and not be hungry any more.

FISH WOMAN: (*Off.*) Fish for sale! Fresh and lovely! Sardines! Fresh from the sea!

Immediately a crowd of people appears, jostling and fighting. A sea of elbows. Grim, thin-lipped people, full of need. They are all carrying wheelbarrows of money, weighed down by bricks.

(*Loving it.*) Sardeeeeeeeeeens! Fresh sardeeeeeeeeens! Only forty thousand lire the dozen!

RAPUNZEL: Could you spare me a sardine?

FISH WOMAN: I don't think so love. Sardeeeeens! Forty thousand lire!

RAPUNZEL: That's so expensive!

FISH WOMAN: (*Bitter.*) Really? No!

RAPUNZEL: What's going on? I'm a stranger here. Everyone's suffering.

FISH WOMAN: Give me a thousand lire and I'll tell you.

RAPUNZEL: I haven't got a thousand lire.

FISH WOMAN: Well curses to you then. Sardeeeeeeeeeens! Fresh sardeeeeeeeens! Only forty thousand lire the dozen!

A YOUNG WOMAN: That's extortion!

AN OLD MAN: Disgusting!

FISH WOMAN: You want to feed your children? Then give me your money!

OLD MAN: Hoi! Someone pushed me! Someone's taken money from my barrow!

YOUNG WOMAN: (*Indicating RAPUNZEL.*) It was her! That beggar woman! I saw her!

FISH WOMAN: Yes! Thief! Thief! Thief!

EVERYONE: (*Joining in.*) Thief! Thief! Thief!

Everyone starts grabbing for RAPUNZEL. She backs away.

RAPUNZEL: I didn't steal anything!

OLD MAN: Look at that ring! She's not a pauper, she's a miser! Give me that ring to pay for what you stole!

RAPUNZEL: There must be some mistake.

She turns to run, but the YOUNG WOMAN tries to grab her, and knocks into the fish stand. Soon there is a full-scale fight. People are angry. Money is thrown everywhere, and the fish seem to fly through the air as they are knocked from the stand.

People grab for them, then slip on slimy scales. General chaos. The FISH WOMAN is knocked over. People disperse, clutching fish and money as they go, but some pursue RAPUNZEL. She runs and they follow her, and launch themselves on top of her. Everyone's shouting 'Get the ring! Get the Ring!'. RAPUNZEL's running as fast as she can. AMBROSI, drunk and asleep in a ditch, wakes up when he hears the commotion. He hears 'Get the ring! Get the girl! After her!' from far away. He rouses himself.

AMBROSI: (*To us.*) Did someone say 'ring?' Did someone say 'girl?' Oh, please let it be the ring. Please let it be the ring! All I'll have to do is, kill the girl, get the ring, and then I'm done. Woohoo. (*To RAPUNZEL, who's running past, pursued by crowd.*) Oi you! Over here!

He grabs her into the ditch and puts his hand over her mouth. They watch everyone run past. When finally everyone's gone –

RAPUNZEL: Thank you. What's the matter with everyone?

AMBROSI can't keep his eyes off her ring.

AMBROSI: (*To RAPUNZEL.*) You all right? You look a bit peckish. Want a bit of my calzone?

RAPUNZEL: (*Not trusting him one iota, but taking it and eating furiously.*) Thanks.

AMBROSI: Not a bit of it. What brings you to this Godforsaken hole?

RAPUNZEL: I'm looking for someone.

AMBROSI: Who might that be? I know most people of importance in the vicinity.

RAPUNZEL: The person I'm looking for isn't important. Except to me.

AMBROSI: Love thing? I notice you've got an exquisite ring there. Ruby is it?

RAPUNZEL: Mind your own business.

AMBROSI: Have some more calzone.

RAPUNZEL: Thanks.

AMBROSI: So where you headed to?

RAPUNZEL: (*Hoovering up her food.*) The palace. I've got an errand there.

AMBROSI: You might not want to go there at the moment. These are dangerous times.

RAPUNZEL: (*Eating.*) Hmm?

AMBROSI: The Duke's gone doolally, he's spent all the city's money, and people are getting angry.

RAPUNZEL: Why?

AMBROSI: Some trouble with his son.

RAPUNZEL: I don't care. I have to get to the palace.

AMBROSI: Determined, aren't you? I like a bit of determination. A bit of pluck.

RAPUNZEL: Look. You were kind, and if you want me to do a favour for you in return, let me do it quickly now, so I can get to the palace.

AMBROSI: No no no no, no no no no. On the contrary. Giving is its own best reward don't you think?

RAPUNZEL: Not always, no.

AMBROSI: In fact, if you want, I'll show you the way to the palace. Bit out of my way, but what's a few kilometres amongst fellow travellers?

RAPUNZEL: What to do. I don't like this skinny, pock-faced (*Or whatever appropriate disparaging adjectives.*) man but I need his help. Should I go with him? Should I trust him? Hmm, I'll go for it and if the worst comes to the worst, I've got my acorns.

They both walk in silence.

Are we nearly there?

AMBROSI: Not long now.

They both walk and walk. It gets darker. RAPUNZEL begins to suspect that all is not as it seems.

RAPUNZEL: Are we nearly there now?

AMBROSI: Oh, just a little further. Have some tiramisu.

They walk, and they walk, and they walk, until RAPUNZEL can stand no more.

RAPUNZEL: WHERE IS THE PALACE?

AMBROSI: Oh, a mere hop away.

They enter a thick dark forest. RAPUNZEL doesn't get frightened easily, but now her heart begins to beat faster. There are eerie shadows and strange noises.

RAPUNZEL: Where are we?

AMBROSI gets out his gun, points it to her head and ties her to a tree. RAPUNZEL spits at him.

You pathetic, evil little man!

AMBROSI: Don't say that.

AMBROSI raises his gun and tries to shoot RAPUNZEL. But suddenly he finds he can't.

What's the matter with me? Come on Ambrosi, do your stuff.

He raises his gun again.

RAPUNZEL: Guilty conscience?

AMBROSI: Shut up, of course not.

He aims, then vacillates again.

Oh *risi e bisi*, what is going on?

RAPUNZEL: What do you want, anyway?

AMBROSI: Your ring, of course.

RAPUNZEL: You'll never get my ring off me as long as I
live. I promised to keep it close to my heart.

AMBROSI: That's moving.

He raises the gun.

RAPUNZEL: What's wrong, can't you do it?

AMBROSI: Look, shut up. I'm trying to concentrate. I've
had a head injury. Come on Ambrosi. Focus.

He tries again. No luck.

I can't shoot!

RAPUNZEL: Why not? Go on!

AMBROSI: I just can't. I want to, but I can't.

RAPUNZEL: So, untie me then.

AMBROSI: No I can't do that. Look, I'm sorry about this.

*He hits RAPUNZEL on the head with his gun, and she
passes out.*

Sorry. Pathetic. My old man would be turning in his
grave.

*He takes RAPUNZEL's ring and skulks off, shaking his
head.*

SCENE 6

MOTHER GOTHEL in her garden, mixing. She is looking at the plant with the eyes. It looks dishevelled.

GOTHEL: Monkshood, hemlock, belladonna. He still lives, I know he still lives, but only just, he is not thriving. It may not take much to finish him. Look how dark the sky grows. Soon it will blast down on him, with its thunderbolts and flashes. Who would be blind in a storm?

SCENE 7

PATRIZIO walks in the mountains. He is thinner, raggier, dirtier, iller than before.

PATRIZIO: Rapunzel it's strange but I can still feel her, your mother's presence. It's as if she's watching us. But she's welcome to. She won't stop me finding you. I will die rather than stop searching.

A massive storm breaks out. The path on which PATRIZIO is standing breaks, behind and in front of him. He feels it with his stick.

I can't go forward, I can't go back. Every step I take is in the dark, so a leap in the dark is only like a big step. My life is not a life without you, and the dark would not be the dark with you.

He leaps. With the tips of his fingers he manages to scrabble for a hold, and heaves himself up. The sun comes out. He lies there for a moment. He hears a noise off. Someone yelling in pain.

MAN: (*Off.*) Baldraccia! (*Thwack.*) Donnacia! (*Thwack.*) Lucciola! (*Thwack.*)

PREZZEMOLINA: (*Off.*) Per favore, ti devi fermare! Per favore!

PATRIZIO: Hello! Hello!

He stumbles on, and comes upon a man beating a young woman, PREZZEMOLINA.

MAN: Slut! Lazy bag of bones!

PREZZEMOLINA: Per piacere! Please!

PATRIZIO: What's going on?

MAN: Can't you see what's going on? I'm beating this lazy cow.

PATRIZIO: Stop that at once.

MAN: Or what?

PATRIZIO: Or I'll thrash you.

MAN: How many fingers am I holding up? Eh? Eh?

But PATRIZIO gives him a good thwack. They have a punch-up, but PATRIZIO has learnt to listen and is surprisingly good. He suffers a black eye, but knocks the man out.

PATRIZIO: (*Kneeling at the man's side.*) What have I done? I've never hit anyone before. He's not dead is he? Oh good. He's breathing. (*To PREZZEMOLINA.*) Are you okay?

PREZZEMOLINA looks sad.

Come on, we'd better get you out of here before he comes round. What's your name?

PREZZEMOLINA: Prezzemolina.

PATRIZIO: I'm Patrizio. I'm looking for a girl called Rapunzel. Have you seen her?

PREZZEMOLINA shakes head, then remembers he can't see.

PREZZEMOLINA: No.

PATRIZIO: I'm going to go back to the city, see if I can get news of her there. You'll be safer in the city. Would you like me to take you?

PREZZEMOLINA: Yes.

We can see from the way she looks at him that she's rather fallen for him. He's oblivious.

PATRIZIO: Do you know the way to the city?

PREZZEMOLINA: No.

PATRIZIO: If you stand here, can you see any buildings, any castles, in the distance?

PREZZEMOLINA: No.

PATRIZIO: Do you know where we are?

PREZZEMOLINA: I was taken from my village by that man when I was twelve.

PATRIZIO: That's terrible Prezzemolina.

Behind them the MAN has got up and is about to thrash PATRIZIO.

PREZZEMOLINA: Look out!

PATRIZIO turns and they have a good old punch-up. Together, PATRIZIO and PREZZEMOLINA floor him. PREZZEMOLINA goes over.

Now he is really dead.

She stamps on him.

PATRIZIO: Dead? I really didn't mean to kill him. Are you sure he's –

PREZZEMOLINA: You're stronger than you think.

PATRIZIO: We must bury him. That's really wrong, to have killed him Prezze.

They dig.

PATRIZIO: Poor brute. I'm really sorry.

PREZZEMOLINA: Not poor brute. Just brute. Just a horrible violent nasty selfish brute with no speck of humanity left inside him.

PATRIZIO: I hope his soul rests in peace.

PREZZEMOLINA: I hope he rots in hell.

They sprinkle earth on him. PREZZEMOLINA spits.

SCENE 8

The DUKE's chamber. The DUKE, as before, but even stonier looking. An adviser, SIGNOR FARFALLA, is there. PAULO listens in at the door.

DUKE: Update me.

FARFALLA: Eighteen attempts to find Patrizio. Eleven unaccounted for, seven returned with elaborate field findings of the pig. And these are your bills, expenses for the expeditions etc etc.

He spreads out numerous naturalists' drawings of the pig, most looking like dragons or bears, in fact nothing like the real pig. The DUKE picks them up incredulously.

DUKE: What's that?

FARFALLA: An artist's impression of the pig, sire.

DUKE: Can it be so hard to find them?

FARFALLA: Apparently, sire.

DUKE: We must borrow more money. I'll contact the
Duke of Lombardy. He's stinking rich and he owes me
a favour.

FARFALLA: If I may make so bold, sire – the people are
starving. They are beginning to resent you. Borrowing
more money is only a short-term solution.

DUKE: I'm starving too. Starving for sight of my Patrizio.
I have to find him. Stay here whilst I write a letter to
Lombardy. Then do not let it out of your sight until it is
in his sweaty palms.

PAULO bursts in, horrified at the DUKE's plan.

PAULO: Father! Stunning day! How are you?

DUKE: Not good. I'm writing to Lombardy to get him to
lend me money.

PAULO: Lombardy! How odd! I was going to pass by his
emissary later for a game of chess. Why don't *I* take the
letter?

DUKE: Thank you Paulo but it needs to be done
immediately.

PAULO: I'll be back in five minutes. Five. Minutes. Please
don't send the letter until then.

DUKE: Very well, but if you're not back, I will send it with
Signor Farfalla here.

PAULO: Five minutes!

*PAULO runs to his chamber, where AMBROSI is waiting.
PAULO grabs him by the wrist and speaks in an urgent
whisper. This whole exchange is very quick.*

Where's the body? I've got five minutes to stop the
country going bankrupt!

AMBROSI: Sire, I've been everywhere. From Brindisi to Milano, via Rome. No sign of Patrizio. Niente.

PAULO withers him with a look.

PAULO: Why I thought I could trust you, you useless twopenny villain –

AMBROSI: Steady sire. I have something that might interest you.

PAULO: Give it to me!

AMBROSI hands over ring.

It's definitely the one. Nobody could mistake its lustre, its delicacy. Where did you find this?

AMBROSI: A girl, your Highness.

PAULO: Oh vile. Did she know where he was?

AMBROSI: She was looking for him herself.

PAULO: And you killed her, of course.

AMBROSI: Naturally.

PAULO: And you brought me her body so that we could use it as evidence.

AMBROSI: No. It was too smooth and girlish. But I *have* brought this.

He shows a skull.

PAULO: That's a sheep's skull.

AMBROSI: Yes.

PAULO: And that helps us how?

AMBROSI: I thought it would add to the veracity of our tale.

PAULO: (*Beside himself with fury but with no time to act on it.*) Idiot. Come on. We've got to do better than this. Now where's that costume?

He rummages in a box.

Put this on.

He gives AMBROSI a peasant woman costume.

AMBROSI: Ha ha ha. Good one.

PAULO fixes him with an icy stare.

You're serious.

PAULO: I most certainly am. Put it on.

AMBROSI: I can't.

PAULO: We've got three minutes left to save the kingdom! Put it on.

AMBROSI struggles to put it on. The effect is somewhat ridiculous.

Good. Excellent. Your name is Sylvia and you are a peasant. Now we just need the bone you found whilst searching for mushrooms in the forest.

Sequence of finding things to be the hand: twigs, sausages, the more ridiculous the better. They get more desperate. The clock ticks. Finally...

Cut off my finger.

AMBROSI: NO!

PAULO: Cut it off!

AMBROSI: No way.

PAULO: Very well.

He takes his sword and cuts off his ring finger. AMBROSI is astonished.

Well? What are you waiting for!

Staunching the flow with a cloth, PAULO and AMBROSI rush to the DUKE's chamber. PAULO, in considerable pain, and dripping blood, bursts in, followed by AMBROSI dressed as Sylvia.

Father, I'm sorry to interrupt your letter-writing. I have urgent news. Please, sit down. Speak, woman.

AMBROSI: Your Reverence, your Majesty. Words cannot do justice to the extremity of emotion I am feeling. I will let objects speak for themselves.

He hands a parcel to the DUKE, containing PAULO's finger and the ring.

DUKE: What is it?

PAULO: Open it, father.

The DUKE slowly opens the parcel.

DUKE: No! No! Patrizio!

He collapses into a chair, and kisses the finger and the ring.

DUKE: Patrizio! (*Trying to compose himself.*) Tell me, peasant, how you came to find him.

AMBROSI: Sire, I am a humble peasant, eking out a meagre existence picking fungi from the forest. Early one morning, I was out foraging when I heard the plaintive cries of one of my goatkids. Maaaa! Maaaaaa!

PAULO gives him a dirty look, as if to say, 'Don't overdo it sonny boy'.

I went to rescue the poor animal, which was caught in the thorny branches of a bush. As I bent low to untangle

it, I saw a pile of white bones. I thought nothing of it
– death is everywhere in the forest, but then the rays of
the morning sun breathed on the bones and illuminated
them, and I saw something glowing and flickering.
It was so beautiful I couldn't breathe sire, but I went
nearer to see what it was. And the rest you know sire. I
was shocked and devastated to discover –

DUKE: My son's ring. Patrizio! I was so convinced that you
were alive, so looking forward to seeing you again. Each
night I dream of you and it is as though you are here
with me again. Can this be so? Can you be dead, who is
so alive in me? Patrizio!

PAULO: I'm so very sorry father.

DUKE: (*Ignoring him.*) Sound the trumpets. Let all wear
black and mourn. Let the funeral be forthwith, and
afterwards, I will cast off my crown, and seek my own
death.

The DUKE exits.

PAULO: You did well. We might have more sport for you
presently.

AMBROSI: Thank you.

PAULO: One more thing. You're quite sure the girl is dead?

AMBROSI: What do you take me for?

PAULO: Good. In that case you won't mind if I ask you to
bring me her body.

SCENE 9

*The forest, where RAPUNZEL was left. Night-time. Strange calls of
owls and wolves. RAPUNZEL slowly comes to in the forest.*

RAPUNZEL: Aaagh, my head!

She spits out earth. Looks around her. Suddenly realises the ring is gone. Panics and curses. She manages to free her hands, and then discovers in one of her pockets one of the acorns.

What if... Could I... Is now the time? I don't know. Should I? All right. Let's go for it. I've got nothing to lose, everything to gain.

She takes one of the acorns and throws it on the ground. Strange music. A suit of men's clothes, seemingly dancing, moving on its own, enters. RAPUNZEL is amazed and entranced.

Wonderful!

RAPUNZEL puts them on. They fit her perfectly. Then a pair of shoes comes, and a hat. They too fit perfectly.

Sunrise.

To the palace!

And she sets off on her way to find the city.

Interval.

SCENE 10

The funeral. A mournful trumpet sounds. People dressed in black, looking glum, scurry past. In his chamber, the DUKE is looking dignified but bereft. He is dressed in black. Beside him is a coffin. It is a full-sized coffin, but in it is the finger of PRINCE PAULO, and the ring. SIGNOR FARFALLA is there.

DUKE: Is all ready?

FARFALLA: Yes your Majesty.

DUKE: Who will bear the coffin?

FARFALLA: The Prince and myself sire.

DUKE: Good. Open the doors. Let the people come in.

The STAFF of the palace line up to pay respects to PRINCE PATRIZIO. Some have rosaries, some have gifts. There is an air of utter solemnity; some silent tears. Last, behind them, is PAULO, his face in a rigid mask of false grief. Before he reaches the coffin, an elderly lady, a COOK, who deeply loved PATRIZIO, breaks down as she looks down at the finger.

COOK: God rest his soul who was taken so savagely from this earth!

She is in paroxysms of tears. The DUKE takes her by the hand and looks stonily on as PAULO genuflects in front of the coffin.

I am very sorry for your loss sir

PAULO: Thank you. He is with the angels now.

DUKE: And now, friends, let the procession begin.

'The Duke's Song':

> Fool, if you pour all your gold into one coffer,
> It might be stolen.
>
> Fool, if you chase the things you love,
> They might take flight.
>
> Fool, if you grow too fond,
> Your heart might break.
>
> Fool, if you plant all your seed into one furrow,
> It might get eaten.
>
> Fool, if you try to train your vine,
> It might wither and die.
>
> Fool, if you cling onto hope when
> There is none,
> It will elude you.

Solemn music. PAULO, still in agony, and SIGNOR FAR-FALLA pick up the coffin and exit the palace, followed by the palace mourners. In the streets, all is quiet. A couple of people watch the procession and genuflect as it passes. The procession passes solemnly. The DUKE is beyond grief. At the church door, a PRIEST greets the procession and sprinkles the coffin with holy water. The procession enters the church.

The road to the city.

RAPUNZEL: Soon I'll be with you Patrizio, I'll be kissing you, holding you, loving you, begging your forgiveness! Even though I don't have the ring any more, I still feel you close to me. Look! The city gates!

A sad bell tolls.

There's no one around. It's so quiet, so mournful.

Finally, a MAN WITH A PARCEL crosses the square.

Please help me. I need to find the palace. I'm looking for a friend.

MAN WITH PARCEL: I'm going there now, take these pastries for the wake.

RAPUNZEL: Who's died?

MAN WITH PARCEL: The youngest Prince.

RAPUNZEL and the MAN WITH PARCEL walk in silence towards the palace. As they pass the church, the funeral procession is leaving. They have no choice but to follow the mourners. RAPUNZEL and the MAN WITH PARCEL follow the mourners, who are singing. The singing continues over the following conversation.

RAPUNZEL: (*In a whisper.*) It seems he was much loved.

MAN WITH PARCEL: The only decent one among them.

RAPUNZEL: May he rest in peace.

They walk in silence. The party comes to the palace churchyard. The PRIEST sprinkles more holy water.

PRIEST: Memento Domine, famulorum famularumque
tuarum Patrizio qui nos praecesserunt cum signo fidei,
et dormiunt in somno pacis. Ipsis, Domine, et omnibus
in Christo quiescentibus, locum refrigerii, lucis et pacis,
ut indulgeas, deprecamur. Per eumdem Christum
Dominum nostrum. Amen.

*The coffin is lowered into the ground. Everyone stands with
bowed heads.*

DUKE: Today we bury the brightest light of our kingdom,
and as that light is rested in the earth, so I renounce
my title and my wealth and go and seek to understand
why this is so. I have caused you, my people, much
suffering, vainly spending your money in my attempts
to find him. I leave you now in the capable hands of my
remaining son Paulo.

There is an outcry.

PEOPLE: Don't leave us sire! Don't abdicate! Don't
let those blockheads take over! Help us rebuild our
community! Help us! Help us sire!

A COUPLE OF DETRACTORS: Good! You ruined us! You
destroyed us! Now it's your turn to suffer!

PAULO: Silence! Let my father finish speaking!

DUKE: Thank you. Thank you my people, many of you
loyal against all hope, loyal when I have punished you
to your limits. I know many of you have lost loved ones,
and why should I be different? I believe losing Patrizio
is my punishment for trying so hard to find him.

RAPUNZEL: Patrizio? It must be a popular name.

MEMBER OF CROWD: Shh.

*There are murmurs from the crowd, some in support of the
DUKE, some against him.*

DUKE: I love Patrizio. He would have been my heir. I wanted him to rule you, wisely and fairly. I'm not asking for your pity, but I am suffering as you have all suffered. Patrizio was savaged by a wild pig in the forest.

Gasps from those that did not know this.

Since I have discovered this, waking or dreaming, I am on that mountain with him and also being ripped from limb to limb and savaged. My hours are full of blood and terror.

RAPUNZEL: Poor man!

DUKE: My last wish is that you work with my son Paulo to try and rebuild this city. Abandon vengeance. And remember my son.

He unveils a portrait of PATRIZIO.

RAPUNZEL: No! Patrizio!

She sinks to her knees. The DUKE puts on a black cloak and exits, regal to the last. PAULO sees RAPUNZEL prostrate with grief.

PAULO: (*To FARFALLA.*) Oh look over there, a boy genuinely overcome with grief. I must have him watched. I do not want any fans of Patrizio, or my father, left in the palace.

FARFALLA: Very well your Highness.

RAPUNZEL is in a heap on the floor, weeping. AMBROSI enters through the audience, looking them up and down.

AMBROSI: Excuse me, has anyone seen a woman, 'bout yea high, funny clothes, no hair to speak of, sparky, spirited, pain in the neck? Anyone? I absolutely have to find her. You sure? No? I left her at the third oak on the left, but when I got there, nothing. I can't believe she escaped, I'm brilliant at knots. (*To audience.*) You look observant. Have you seen her? No? You're certain? Please? Come on, someone must have seen her.

Maybe someone says she's dressed as a man. Improvise with what the audience says.

I am going to be in the total *merda*. I know Shark Fantini knows I'm back. Oh, it's arriver-blimmin-derci to my country life if I don't find her.

PAULO glides past.

PAULO: Ah, Ambrosi. Do you have a body for us?

AMBROSI: Yes, yes, it's all under control.

PAULO: Bring it to my chambers in ten minutes.

PAULO glides off. SHARK FANTINI shines a torch into the audience.

SHARK FANTINI: Anyone seen that scum Ambrosi?

AMBROSI sits on someone's lap in the audience and stays very still.

Come on, has anyone seen him? I'm going to kill him! I told him to keep away from the city, but he's been seen sniffing around that sinister Prince Paulo! I'm going to get him!

AMBROSI: (*Shivering on someone's lap.*) Shhh. Please shhhh.

The audience may or may not betray him. If they do:

'AMBROSI: Thanks a lot, friends – ' as he dashes out of the auditorium, swiftly followed by SHARK FANTINI. Gunshots are heard off.

If they don't:

SHARK FANTINI enters the audience and starts looking for AMBROSI. AMBROSI changes position a few times etc. Improvise with the same ending.

The palace. AMBROSI enters dragging the body of SHARK FANTINI.

Well. I have a body. It doesn't look much like the girl, granted. But it is a body. And if I leave it in this sack, d'you think, maybe, I'll have time to escape before Paulo finds out? I've had enough of all this. I don't even care about the gold any more. I crave peace. I'm out of here. To the mountains!

He drags the body to the chamber of PRINCE PAULO. SIGNOR FARFALLA is there.

Delivery for Prince Paulo. Guard it with your life. Tell him I'll see him later.

And he's off.

FARFALLA: Very well.

RAPUNZEL alone, weeping, walks off. When she has gone, PAULO comes back.

The youth has gone.

PAULO: Why weren't you quicker, jellyfish? We can't afford slackness at any time.

FARFALLA: I had to guard this.

PAULO: Ah, the body. Fantastic. Let's look upon this woman, and laugh at the kind of hussy that attracted our brother.

PAULO lifts the sheet off the body, to reveal a dead SHARK FANTINI.

She's not very attractive. Oh. It's King Shark Fantini. What? Has Ambrosi disobeyed me? The viper! We will scour the countryside and find him. My first act as Duke will be to kill Ambrosi, display his head for all to see that traitors will be shown no mercy.

SCENE 11

MOTHER GOTHEL mixing a potion in her garden. The eye-bush is by her side.

GOTHEL: Wormwood, thyme, tansy. Monkshood, lovage, orach.

My pretty Rapunzel, where are you? Are you coming back to me to say sorry mother, sorry, I was headstrong and bold? Are you coming back to look after my old bones and make me a tisane from time to time? Will you tend me in my dotage? Will you dress me like your dolly when I am old and like a child again? Sweetheart?

She sprinkles the mixture on the ground. She sees RAPUNZEL, dressed as a boy.

RAPUNZEL: Patrizio. Can it be true that you are dead love? It cannot be. I will go around the world to find you, any part of you, even your dead bones.

She goes off up the track into the distance. She walks, clearly grief-stricken. GOTHEL is shocked.

GOTHEL: That fine shrub daily reproaches me with a million eyes. He is not yet dead. But she thinks he's dead. She's unsure of herself – but so determined! Why Gothel, why did you teach her so well? I must find a way of killing him forever in her heart. Nature – I have tended you, nurtured you, helped you blossom and thrive in this desert land. Can you help me now?

She looks in her book.

'To destroy a love stronger than death.' Succory, orach, oregano – turn me into a false Patrizio.

She changes herself into a FALSE PATRIZIO.

End of Act Two.

Act Three

SCENE 1

Morning.

RAPUNZEL: (*Walking in the mountains.*) I'll go on and find you. My love is stronger than death. My love is stronger than pain. My love is stronger than hunger. Patrizio! Patrizio!

She hears the ting-a-ling of a bell. A GOAT scampers across the rocks. PIERLUIGI AMBROSI follows, chatting to his GOAT.

AMBROSI: Allay, allay, Mirabel. How lovely to be here. Away from all the brouhaha.

The GOAT baas soulfully. RAPUNZEL recognises AMBROSI and freezes. Slowly her demeanour changes from grief-stricken to furious.

Yes, I know I done wrong. And I'm sure one day I'll have to pay for it. I never meant the old Duke no 'arm, nor the Prince Patrizio neither. As for the girl…

The GOAT baas.

RAPUNZEL: You! It's you! It's all your fault!

She flies at him.

AMBROSI: I don't know what you're talking about.

RAPUNZEL: You! You made this happen!

AMBROSI: I don't think I've had the pleasure.

RAPUNZEL: Oh really?

She casts her hat off, then floors him.

AMBROSI: (*On the floor.*) Oh. It's you.

RAPUNZEL: (*Putting her foot on his neck.*) Where's my ring? Where's Patrizio?

AMBROSI: I can't tell you. It's too complicated.

RAPUNZEL: (*Squeezing with her foot.*) Try, or I'll asphyxiate you very slowly with my foot.

AMBROSI: (*Unable to breathe.*) Prince Paulo wanted to be Duke because he is a power-hungry psycho but also to be fair because the old Duke was bankrupting the country so he asked me to prove that Prince Patrizio was dead because that was the condition on which the old Duke said he would abdicate the throne and I had to get the ring to prove to the Duke that Prince Patrizio was dead.

RAPUNZEL: So you don't know if Prince Patrizio is alive or dead? It was just a scam to dupe the Duke?

AMBROSI: Correct.

RAPUNZEL: Your mum must be proud of you earning your money like that.

AMBROSI: I didn't take all the money.

RAPUNZEL: I knew he was alive! You're so pathetic. Hasn't anyone ever taught you that what you do affects other people? Are you willing to make amends, or shall I kill you?

AMBROSI: Let's see.

RAPUNZEL: You're not in a position to make jokes.

AMBROSI: I'm in, I'm in. Now get off me.

She gets off him.

Which way are we going?

RAPUNZEL: I don't know. I don't know where he is – I don't even know if he's on the mountains. But I will scour every centimetre of this land until I find him.

AMBROSI: T'riffic.

RAPUNZEL: Get up. We've no time to lose.

SCENE 2

PAULO on horseback, with SIGNOR FARFALLA, pursued by midges.

PAULO: This is ridiculous. We've been searching the mountains for days. All we've seen – is *wildlife*. Get off me you filthy little – ! Aaagh! Ouch!

Baa, baa. And human voices off.

AMBROSI: Cut us a bit of slack, would you?

RAPUNZEL: Hurry up! We're not on a lovely alpine stroll!

PAULO and FARFALLA get out their guns as goats walk on, followed by AMBROSI and RAPUNZEL. RAPUNZEL is focused on only one thing, finding PATRIZIO. AMBROSI lags behind. They have not seen PAULO and FARFALLA. Suddenly, AMBROSI and RAPUNZEL are face to face with PAULO and FARFALLA. They stop dead. AMBROSI is the first to recover his composure.

AMBROSI: Your Highness! What a lovely morning for an alpine stroll!

PAULO: Seize them!

FARFALLA ties AMBROSI and RAPUNZEL.

Pierluigi Ambrosi, you are a traitor to myself and by extension the Kingdom of Tuscany.

AMBROSI: How so, Excellency?

PAULO: You were supposed to slay the girl, not Shark Fantini.

AMBROSI: I know, I know, your Highness, I apologise, it got a bit complicated. As it happens, I was just bringing you the girl.

Subtle nudging of RAPUNZEL.

RAPUNZEL: I'm her brother.

AMBROSI: Yes, this is um, Fulvio.

PAULO: Fulvio? You were blubbing at my brother's funeral. Did you know him?

RAPUNZEL: (*Reaching in her pocket for a magic acorn.*) Yes, we were in a mandolin ensemble together as children.

PAULO: How moving. Take me to your sister.

RAPUNZEL: If you untie us.

PAULO: I'm not stupid. Take me to her and then I will untie you.

RAPUNZEL: Of course your Highness.

RAPUNZEL manages to wriggle her fingers down into her pocket and gets out a magic acorn. She throws it. Immediately chaos. A thick mist descends. They all cough. When the mist clears, FARFALLA, PAULO and the horse have all been changed into RABBITS, which hop off. One RABBIT has an injured paw.

He won't bother us again.

AMBROSI: Who taught you to do that?

RAPUNZEL: A pig.

AMBROSI: A pig. Right.

They walk on for a while.

A disembodied voice.

VOICE: Rapunzel!

RAPUNZEL: Did you hear that?

VOICE: Rapunzel!

RAPUNZEL: It's him! It's Patrizio! Patrizio I'm coming!

She runs towards the voice. AMBROSI struggles to keep up with her.

VOICE: (*From other direction.*) Rapunzel! Rapunzel!

RAPUNZEL: Where are you?

VOICE: Rapunzel! I'm here!

RAPUNZEL: I'm coming!

AMBROSI: I don't like this.

We see the FALSE PATRIZIO, sitting on a rock.

RAPUNZEL: Patrizio! Is it you?

GOTHEL / FALSE PATRIZIO: Yes.

RAPUNZEL: Oh my love.

She runs to him. She kneels at his feet and weeps.

Patrizio. I'm sorry. I should have trusted you. I should have been more patient. This is all my fault.

GOTHEL / FALSE PATRIZIO: It's all right Rapunzel. I'm here now. Everything is all right.

AMBROSI: Rapunzel!

RAPUNZEL: What is it?

AMBROSI: Come away from him.

RAPUNZEL: What are you talking about?

AMBROSI: I dunno, I've got a funny feeling about this. Something ain't right.

RAPUNZEL: You're just jealous!

AMBROSI: No. I just don't think it's him.

RAPUNZEL: Oh, go and look after your goats. You've caused enough trouble round here already. Patrizio! It's me!

She goes to embrace the FALSE PATRIZIO, but he repels her.

GOTHEL / FALSE PATRIZIO: Do you think I still really want you, you raggedy bag of bones? You let me go, you couldn't even wait for me for three weeks, and now you expect me to take you back?

RAPUNZEL is stunned.

RAPUNZEL: Patrizio I'm so sorry. I've learned my lesson. I've been everywhere looking for you, everywhere, for months, my heart is sore from missing you.

GOTHEL / FALSE PATRIZIO: Oh poor you. Why did you cut all your hair off? It looks terrible!

RAPUNZEL: Patrizio why are you being so cruel? I know you've had hard times, but –

GOTHEL / FALSE PATRIZIO: Because you are a wicked, selfish girl.

He goes to overpower her. She fights him.

RAPUNZEL: I'm not! I'm not! What's come over you? Who's done this to you? Why are you being like this?

GOTHEL / FALSE PATRIZIO: (*In MOTHER GOTHEL's voice.*) You have hurt me so much my darling. Won't you come back to mother?

RAPUNZEL: No! Go away!

GOTHEL: You won't get to him you know. He's probably fallen into a ravine.

RAPUNZEL: You're evil!

GOTHEL: I'll see you soon, my darling, back in our garden. Don't be long. I'll be waiting.

She goes. RAPUNZEL breaks down into sobs. AMBROSI tries to comfort her.

AMBROSI: It's all right. It's all right.

RAPUNZEL: No, it's not. I'll never find him. She'll always be there to stop me. I should just give up, and go home.

AMBROSI: Don't take on. I'll help you. I promise.

RAPUNZEL: I can't go on.

AMBROSI: Don't you see that's what she wants, for you to give up?

RAPUNZEL: I don't care any more.

AMBROSI: Now steady on, what happened to the little tiger who nearly knocked my block off a few hours ago? Don't tell me that was all a sham?

RAPUNZEL: Leave me.

AMBROSI: Never.

A song in which AMBROSI tries to encourage RAPUNZEL.

> When you have a wall to lean on
> There's no need to fall down.
>
> When you have a map stretched out
> You do not have to lose yourself.
>
> For even the night
> Is not the night
> When you love is near.

Even the night
Is not the night
When the darkness holds the sun inside.

When you have a well to drink from
Don't let your lips be parched.

When you have porter for your bag
Let his arms take the strain.

For even the night is not the night
When your love is near.
Even the night is not the night
When the darkness holds the sun inside.

He helps her up and they walk off together.

SCENE 3

Evening. PREZZEMOLINA and PATRIZIO walk on. PREZZE-MOLINA is addled with love for PATRIZIO.

PREZZEMOLINA: Patrizio. Have you ever wondered what it would be like to kiss me?

PATRIZIO: No.

PREZZEMOLINA: You don't like me?

PATRIZIO: I do, I do, you're lovely. We've been good friends, no?

PREZZEMOLINA: I love you.

PATRIZIO: Please. Prezze. Don't. I love Rapunzel.

PREZZEMOLINA: If she loved you, she would have found you by now.

PATRIZIO: Maybe. Maybe she doesn't love me any more. But I have to find out. I have to find her.

PREZZEMOLINA: You'd be better off with someone who does.

PATRIZIO: You could be right, Prezze, but I have to know.

PREZZEMOLINA: We could lie down right here and have a cuddle.

PATRIZIO: We could.

PREZZEMOLINA: You only met her twice.

PATRIZIO: Yes.

PREZZEMOLINA: And one of those times she wasn't nice to you.

PREZZEMOLINA goes to cuddle him. He's only human, but –

PATRIZIO: But there would be no point. I will always love her. Always, Prezze.

She nuzzles up to him.

Stop it!

He pushes her away.

PREZZEMOLINA: You're just like my husband! Violent! A bully! Help! Help!

PREZZEMOLINA sees a huge SNAKE coming towards them. She stands well back and allows PATRIZIO to approach it.

PATRIZIO: I'm sorry. Don't do that. I'm sorry Prezze.

PREZZEMOLINA watches as the SNAKE goes towards him.

Prezze? Prezze?

She suddenly grabs him.

PREZZEMOLINA: I can't do it.

PATRIZIO: What?

PREZZEMOLINA: There's a snake. I was going to let it bite you.

PATRIZIO: Really.

PREZZEMOLINA: But I changed my mind.

PATRIZIO: Thank you.

PREZZEMOLINA: What shall we do?

PATRIZIO: Carry on, of course.

They walk on, giving the SNAKE a wide berth, and it slinks off in the other direction.

SCENE 4

Back in MOTHER GOTHEL's garden.

GOTHEL: (*Staggering.*) You see how weak I am, Rapunzel? You see how your cruelty is making me frail? I feel spent. I have only one spell left in me. If I can't have you, then no one shall have you. If I cannot see your face – open and trusting like a flower – then no one shall see it. I gave you life. If I hadn't tended you when you were a scrawny scrap of purple, yelling and spewing under the Rapunzel bush, you would not be here now. As I gave you life, so I shall take it away. Rocks, earth, moss, fall upon her as she reaches him.

SCENE 5

Early Morning. Mist. The opposite side of the ravine from PREZZEMOLINA and PATRIZIO. AMBROSI and RAPUNZEL.

RAPUNZEL: When I was a little girl, I worshipped her. She was a goddess to me. She taught me everything. And

78

then suddenly, when I was about fourteen – wham! She put me in a tower. To keep me safe, she said. She didn't want to share me with anyone else. Only there are some things you can't do with a mother. Are you all right?

AMBROSI: Never better.

They walk in silence. The mist lifts to reveal PATRIZIO and PREZZEMOLINA, asleep together, across a huge ravine from them.

RAPUNZEL: Oh look! Pierluigi! He's there! Patrizio is there! It's definitely him! But who's that woman with him? Patrizio!

PATRIZIO: (*Waking.*) What? Who was that?

Finds PREZZEMOLINA tangled up in him. PREZZE-MOLINA remains asleep. PATRIZIO moves away. MOTHER GOTHEL enters and stands a little distance away.

RAPUNZEL: (*To AMBROSI.*) I can't believe it! He's got another woman! The cheek of it!

PATRIZIO: Rapunzel! Is that really you?

RAPUNZEL: Yes, it's me! Oh Patrizio it is you?

PATRIZIO: Yes.

RAPUNZEL: Not mother? If you're mother, just tell me now.

PATRIZIO: No I'm definitely not your mother!

RAPUNZEL: Where's the acorn? I can't find it anywhere!

AMBROSI: Calm down. Look for it carefully.

PATRIZIO: Who's that with you?

RAPUNZEL: My friend Ambrosi.

PATRIZIO: Your friend?

RAPUNZEL: Yes. And who's that person with you?

PATRIZIO: My friend Prezze.

RAPUNZEL: Your friend.

PATRIZIO: Yes.

RAPUNZEL: Oh where's that acorn? Please don't be lost, please. Here it is. Here. Patrizio, I'm coming…

RAPUNZEL gets ready to throw the acorn.

GOTHEL: Don't throw the acorn, pretty.

RAPUNZEL: Go away!

GOTHEL: Don't throw the acorn. I love you better than he does.

RAPUNZEL: No.

GOTHEL: You think that pup can love you as I do? That blind pup? My love is higher than the heavens and deeper than the earth.

RAPUNZEL: I love him mother. You have no power over me.

She throws the acorn. As RAPUNZEL throws the acorn, a colourful cloud creates a bridge over the ravine, the earth crumbles away around it, falling on MOTHER GOTHEL, who is crushed to death, and AMBROSI, who is injured. But RAPUNZEL doesn't notice.

I'm coming.

RAPUNZEL reaches the other side. She approaches PATRIZIO and sees he is blind.

Patrizio? You can't see!

PATRIZIO: I know it's you Rapunzel.

RAPUNZEL: It's me.

RAPUNZEL embraces him, weeps, and PATRIZIO's blind eyes can see. They embrace long and passionately.

PATRIZIO: Rapunzel.

PREZZEMOLINA wakes up. She watches them embracing passionately. PATRIZIO and RAPUNZEL walk back across the colourful cloud, glued together. When they get to the other side, the cloud disappears. But then so does the ravine. PREZZEMOLINA just walks across. She notices MOTHER GOTHEL's shoes under some rubble.

PREZZEMOLINA: So, your mother won't be bothering you any more.

RAPUNZEL: Oh!

PATRIZIO: I'm sorry Rapunzel.

RAPUNZEL: I know. I'm sorry too.

She scrapes away some of the rubble. There is a plant growing there.

I think this is her. You'll have to come with us mother.

She puts on her shoes.

Where's Pierluigi? Where is he?

She rushes about the rubble, looking for him. Eventually she finds him. AMBROSI is prone.

What happened? Are you all right?

AMBROSI doesn't move.

Pierluigi! Pierluigi!

He is motionless.

Oh no!

She weeps. PATRIZIO holds her.

81

He was the truest friend anyone could ever have! I would never have found you without him! I loved him more than anyone, except you!

AMBROSI: (*Sitting up.*) Don't shoot!

RAPUNZEL: You vagabond!

She tears a rag off from her jacket and binds his leg with it.

PREZZEMOLINA: I'll do it.

RAPUNZEL: No, it's okay.

PREZZEMOLINA: I'll do it.

PREZZEMOLINA binds his leg tenderly, then supporting AMBROSI, they begin to walk. AMBROSI winces at each step. PATRIZIO is glued to RAPUNZEL. They walk.

A few days later. Sunrise at the city gates. PREZZEMOLINA and AMBROSI are some way behind RAPUNZEL and PATRIZIO.

RAPUNZEL: I'm sorry about turning Paulo into a rabbit. But he was going to kill us.

PATRIZIO: It's partly my fault.

RAPUNZEL: How?

PATRIZIO: A stubborn refusal to see that he was jealous. I always pretended everything was sweet and light.

RAPUNZEL: Thank goodness for the pig.

PATRIZIO: Yes. Praise the pig! I want to thank that pig with all my heart.

A cry of pain from behind them. AMBROSI and PREZZE-MOLINA are sitting down. PREZZEMOLINA has her arm around AMBROSI, which RAPUNZEL still can't quite allow.

RAPUNZEL: I'm so sorry Pierluigi. We're walking too quickly. Here, have a compress.

AMBROSI: Don't give me any more herbs Rapunzel! I can't stand the smell of any more herbs! Just chop it off! Please! I'm in agony!

PREZZEMOLINA: He's in agony. He doesn't want any more herbs.

RAPUNZEL: Just rub this lavender into your thigh. It will help till we get to the palace.

She rubs lavender into his thigh.

AMBROSI: Ow! I'm going to get you for this!

They walk, as before, with AMBROSI supported by PREZZE-MOLINA, and PATRIZIO with RAPUNZEL.

PATRIZIO: Look! The city!

RAPUNZEL / PREZZEMOLINA: So beautiful!

AMBROSI: It's still standing then, just about.

In rags and scarcely recognisable, the four of them stand there. A CITIZEN carrying bread crosses the stage, then sees them and does a double-take.

CITIZEN: I must be seeing things. Prince Patrizio! Ambrosi! And a beautiful boy and girl! All at the city gates!

The CITIZEN goes to strike AMBROSI.

AMBROSI: Ow!

PATRIZIO: Leave him alone, he's with us.

CITIZEN: What a turn up. That's something I never expected to see.

The man rushes to tell people. Soon there is a crowd of people milling about them, telling them what's been going on. RAPUNZEL listens with interest.

It's been chaos and mayhem sire. Total anarchy. Law and order has totally broken down.

General clamour as people talk over each other excitedly.

PATRIZIO: Where's my father?

MAN: When he thought you dead, he retreated to a cell beneath the city. He has seen no one since that day.

PATRIZIO: Take me there.

RAPUNZEL: And me, I'm coming too.

PATRIZIO: Don't you want to get ready for the wedding?

RAPUNZEL: Not yet.

SCENE 6

Music. PATRIZIO and RAPUNZEL walk with a key to find the DUKE. PATRIZIO and RAPUNZEL begin to dig. Eventually the matted hair and earth-encrusted face of the DUKE are revealed. PATRIZIO and RAPUNZEL pull him up by the shoulders and lift him out of the earth. The DUKE is reborn. He blinks blindly into the light. RAPUNZEL and PATRIZIO place him gently in a wheelchair and wheel him off.

SCENE 7

RAPUNZEL is transformed. Women fuss and cluck around her; gauzy fabrics; she is scrubbed and washed and anointed and enrobed in a magnificent dress. She looks extraordinary. Her hair is still resolutely short.

SCENE 8

The wedding. RAPUNZEL, the DUKE in his wheelchair, and PATRIZIO stand there. Everyone is completely jubilant.

PATRIZIO: Thanks everyone for coming. It's so fantastic to be back here amongst my people, and with my father, and my wonderful, courageous, beautiful, fierce, fantastic, mesmerizing Rapunzel. We are going to get married in a minute, but we're just waiting for something and someone very important.

AMBROSI, covered in mud, and on crutches with a bandaged leg, carrying something, followed by PREZZEMOLINA, arrives.

AMBROSI: Even an injured ruffian has no respite. Here's your ring. I've exhumed it! Let the wedding commence!

A PRIEST marries them. Music. Then cheers and hurrahs from all as RAPUNZEL and PATRIZIO are borne aloft by wildly happy citizens. The DUKE is quietly content in his wheelchair. A microphone is passed to the DUKE.

DUKE: We've all had a lot of sorrow and a lot of pain, and for my part in that, I apologise to you all. Now we can be sure that Tuscany will be ruled fairly and honestly by Patrizio with Rapunzel by his side, and I can tend my gardens and watch with pride. So I'd like to introduce my incredible daughter-in-law: Rapunzel.

RAPUNZEL: I'm Rapunzel, and I love this man your Prince Patrizio. We met in unusual circumstances and soon you'll get to hear all about that, but right now I'd just like to introduce myself as your Queen. I can't wait to meet you all. I'm really sorry you've all had such an appalling time, and the first thing we're going to do is look at the tax situation and try and develop our local economy. We have a beautiful city and a stunning region and we're going to regenerate, create jobs, and stop all the corruption. So if you're corrupt you should be quaking in your shoes. I'm going to find out who you are and make you make amends big-style. I'm also going to open a herbalism school in honour of my mother, who was sadly transformed a few weeks ago. She was a fantastic herbalist and she taught me everything I know about plants.

Hurrahs. A RABBIT with an injured forepaw – and a fitter one – lollop dejectedly onto the stage and in front of everyone transform back into PAULO and FARFALLA. Huge whoops of applause and laughter.

And Prince Paulo here is going to be our finance minister, aren't you Prince Paulo? Get these men a drink, they've had a long journey on all fours! I'd just like to publicly give my courageous, handsome, just and incredibly excellent husband his wedding present.

Someone brings on an electric guitar and RAPUNZEL gives it to PATRIZIO.

I'll let you get on with the dancing in a minute, but there's just one more thing I need to do. Where's Ambrosi? Ambrosi, come here. Now I know that you lot know him as a ruffian and ne'er-do-well, but I assure you that he's reformed. I couldn't have found Patrizio without this man. Despite trying to kill me earlier in my adventures, he turned out to be a total diamond and I love him very much. He's going to be my Special Adviser. Thank you Pierluigi.

She presents him with a 'Special Adviser' badge and a massive kiss. PREZZEMOLINA glows with pride mixed with jealousy. Dancing and hurrahs. PREZZEMOLINA tries to get smoochy with AMBROSI but this is left ambivalent...

CITIZEN: There's a huge pig in the palace gardens! Let's slaughter it and have it for the wedding feast!

RAPUNZEL: No!

She runs into the garden, and there is the PIG, with a bouquet.

Thank you!

She gives the PIG a kiss.

'Rapunzel's Theme', led by a tipsy AMBROSI:

ALL: Feels like wine
      Inside our veins
      When first we catch
      A sight of our love.

      Till the moon usurps the sun
      We'll build our home
      Right here with our love.

      No mountain peak or desert land
      Can stop our hearts returning here.
      Our hands will dig in the rich earth
      Our feet will dance here.

      Until the sea engulfs the land
      We'll always be a part of here; our
      Soil will bring good harvest,
      Our bones will settle here.

The End.